PIANO • VOCAL • GUITAR

ULTIMATE

# LATIN SONGS

• 80 HOT HITS •

ISBN 0-634-02180-X

HAL • LEONARD®
CORPORATION

7777 W. BLUEMOUND RD. P.O. BOX 13819 MILWAUKEE, WI 53213

Visit Hal Leonard Online at
www.halleonard.com

# ULTIMATE
# LATIN SONGS

# A ÉSA

Words and Music by MANUEL ALEJANDRO
and MARIA ALEJANDRA

**Additional Lyrics**

2. A ésa,
   Que ahora está, como ya ves
   Destruída de rodar,
   Yo le he escrito mil poemas
   A sus ojos y a su piel.
   *To Chorus*

3. A ésa,
   Le he enseñado a besar,
   A sentir, y a ser mujer,
   Y ya ves que aventajada.
   ¡Quién se lo iba a suponer!
   *To Chorus*

# ACERCATE MÁS
## (Come Closer to Me)

Music and Spanish Words by OSVALDO FARRES
English Words by AL STEWART

# ADIOS

English Words by EDDIE WOODS
Spanish Translation and Music by
ENRIC MADRIGUERA

# ADORO

Words and Music by
ARMANDO MANZANERO CANCHE

# AMOR
## (Amor, Amor, Amor)

Music by GABRIEL RUIZ
Spanish Words by RICARDO LOPEZ MENDEZ
English Words by NORMAN NEWELL

# ALMA CON ALMA

Words and Music by
JUANITO MARQUEZ

24

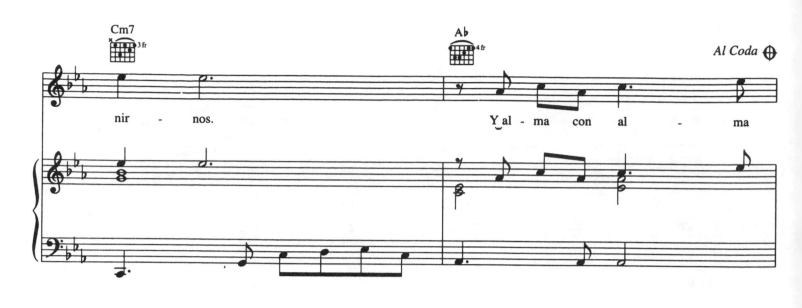

*Al Coda* ⊕

nir - nos.　　　Y al - ma con al - ma

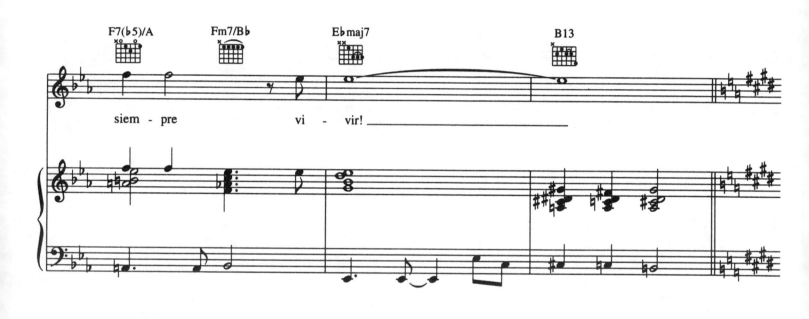

siem - pre　　vi - vir! _____

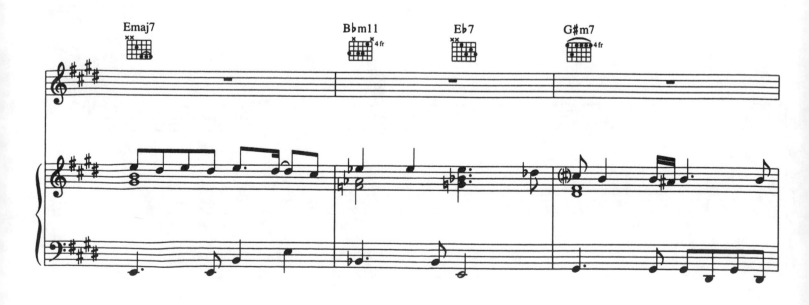

D. S. 𝄋 al Coda

𝄌 Coda

siem - pre        vi - vir!

# ALWAYS IN MY HEART
## (Siempre En Mi Corazón)
from ALWAYS IN MY HEART

Music and Spanish Words by ERNESTO LECUONA
English Words by KIM GANNON

# AMAPOLA
## (Pretty Little Poppy)

By JOSEPH M. LACALLE
New English Words by ALBERT GAMSE

# AMOR ETERNO
## (El Mas Triste Recuerdo)

Words and Music by
JUAN GABRIEL

# ASI FUE

Words and Music by
JUAN GABRIEL

Per - do - na si te ha - go llo - ror
do - na si te cau - so do - lor

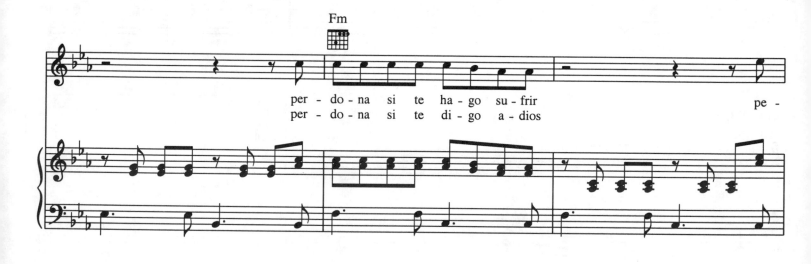

per - do - na si te ha - go su - frir    pe -
per - do - na si te di - go a - dios

ro es que no es - ta en mis ma - nos    pe - ro es que no es - ta en mis
co - mo de - cir - le que te a - mo    co - mo de - cir - le que

# AQUELLOS OJOS VERDES
## (Green Eyes)

Music by NILO MENENDEZ
Spanish Words by ADOLFO UTRERA
English Words by E. RIVIERA AND E. WOODS

Life held no charm, dear, un-til I met you. _____
*Fue - ron tus o - jos los que me die - rón* _____

# BABALÚ

Words and Music by
MARGARITA LECUONA

# BÉSAME MUCHO
## (Kiss Me Much)

Music and Spanish Words by CONSUELO VELAZQUEZ
English Words by SUNNY SKYLAR

# BLAME IT ON THE BOSSA NOVA

Words and Music by BARRY MANN
and CYNTHIA WEIL

I was at a dance _____ when she caught my eye, _____
is my bride to be _____

Stand-in' all a - lone, _____ look-in' sad and shy. _____
And we're gon-na raise _____ a fam-i-ly _____

We be-gan to dance, _____ sway-in' to and fro _____
And when our kids ask _____ how it came a - bout, _____

# BRAZIL

Words and Music by S.K. RUSSELL
and ARY BARROSO

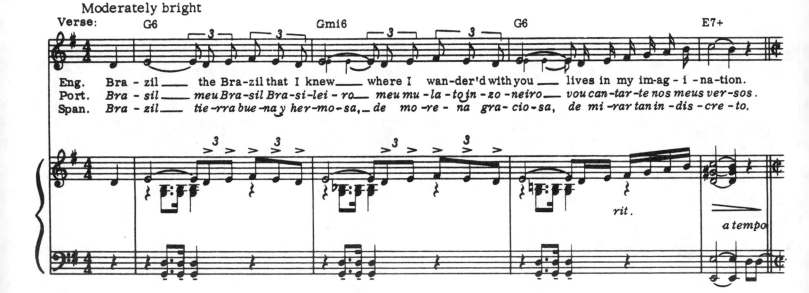

# CACHITA

Words and Music by RAFAEL HERNANDEZ
and BERNARDO SANCRISTOBAL

# CHERRY PINK AND
# APPLE BLOSSOM WHITE

from UNDERWATER

French Words by JACQUES LARUE
English Words by MACK DAVID
Music by LOUIGUY

# THE CONSTANT RAIN
## (Chove Chuva)

Original Words and Music by JORGE BEN
English Words by NORMAN GIMBEL

Cho - ve Chu - va,_____
*Cho - ve Chu - va,_____*

# CASTIGAME

Words and Music by RAFAEL P. BOTIJA,
AENRI QUETA and RAMOS NUNEZ

**Additional Lyrics**

Verse 3:
¿Qué es lo que me pasa esta noche?
¿Qué locura me hizo caer?
Hasta permitir que me lleves,
Com un barco de papel.

Verse 4:
¿Quién seras que todo lo vences,
Y haces lo que quieres de mi?
¿Cómo habra podido entregarme,
Simplemente por decir?

Bridge 2:
Mañana yo me haré por supuesto,
Al verme pensaré. ¿Cómo pude ser de esto?
*To Chorus*

# CORAZON CORAZON

Words and Music by
JOSE MA. NAPOLEON

***Additional Lyrics***

2. Donde vayas he de ir contigo, amor.
   Si una mano necesitas dos tendré,
   Y si sufres una pena,
   Una pena sufriré.
   Cuando rías a tu lado reiré.
   *To Chorus*

3. Cuando nos quedemos solos otra vez,
   Porque tengan nuestros hijios que crecer.
   Tal vez yo te invite al cine.
   Y en lo oscuro como ayer,
   Algun beso en la mejilla te daré.
   *To Chorus*

# COSTUMBRES

Words and Music by
JUAN GABRIEL

**Moderately slow**

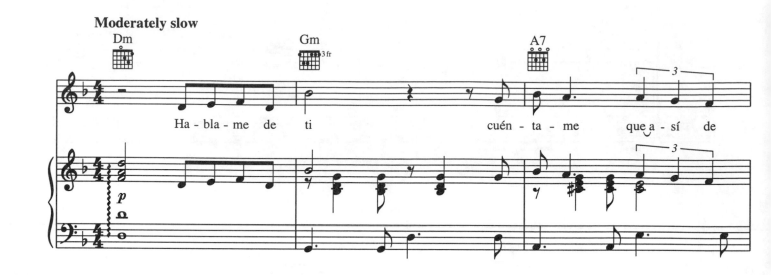

Ha - bla - me de ti          cuén - ta - me que a - sí de

tu oi - do.          Sa - bes tú que sé          que tu es -

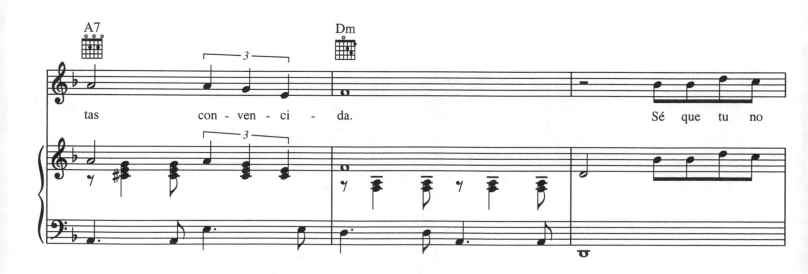

tas con - ven - ci - da.          Sé que tu no

80

# CU-CU-RRU-CU-CU, PALOMA

Words and Music by
THOMAS MENDEZ SOSA

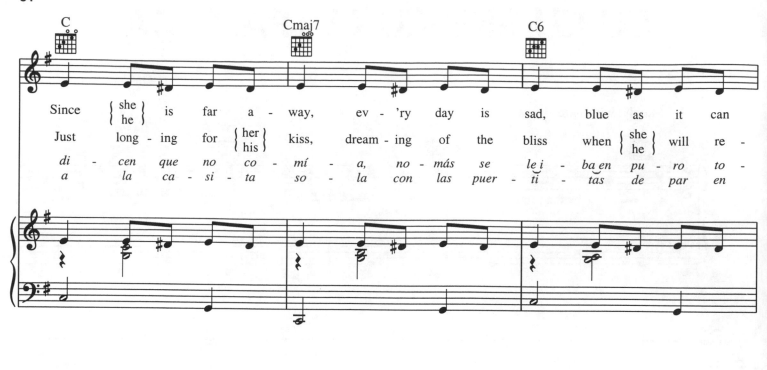

**C**

Since {she/he} is far a - way, ev - 'ry day is sad, blue as it can

Just long - ing for {her/his} kiss, dream - ing of the bliss when {she/he} will re -

*di - cen que no co - mí - a, no - más se le i - ba en pu - ro to -*

*a la ca - si - ta so - la con las puer - ti - tas de par en*

**C**　　**Db**　　**D7**

be;

turn;

*mar;*

*par;*

I could - n't e - ven start pour - ing out my

My head is full of stars, full of soft gui -

*ju - ran que el mis - mo cie - lo se ex - tre - me -*

*ju - ran que e - sa pa - lo - ma no es o - tra*

**G**

heart to {her/him} in a let - ter. _____

tars, full of lov - er's woo - ing. _____

*cí - a al o - ir su llan - to; _____*

*co - ša más que su al - ma, _____*

# CUANTO LE GUSTA

Original Words and Music by GABRIEL RUIZ
English Words by RAY GILBERT

# A DAY IN THE LIFE OF A FOOL
## (Manha De Carnaval)

Words by CARL SIGMAN
Music by LUIZ BONFA

Slowly, with a Bossa Nova beat

A day _____ in the life _____ of a fool, _____
Ma - nhã _____ tão bo - ni - ta ma - nhã. _____

_____ a sad _____ and a long, _____ lone - ly
_____ De um di - a fe - liz _____ que che -

day. _____ I walk the av - e - nue _____
gou. _____ O sol ne céu sur - giu _____

# CUMANA

Words by HAROLD SPINA and ROC HILLMAN
Music by BARCLAY ALLEN

# DINDI

Music by ANTONIO CARLOS JOBIM
Portuguese Lyrics by ALOYSIO de OLIVEIRA
English Lyrics by RAY GILBERT

# EL DESTINO

Words and Music by
JUAN GABRIEL

# EL MEXICO QUE SE NOS FUE

Words and Music by
JUAN GABRIEL

Moderately fast (in one)

Co-mo a cam-bia-do de pue-blo mi pue-blo
Di a sen-con-ta mi no hay l'a-gua de las

ya no es el mis-mo de a
a-ce-qui-as y rios di a

quel tal de
se

pue-blo tan her-mo-so tal de
se-co no hay de a-gua di a se

de a-do-be te es-tan des-a-pa-ra-cien-do

hoy las con-stru-en de blo-que fe - as

las es-ta de sien-do la pla-ta y el o-ro del po-bre

ca - ros se ol-vi-do po-nien-do di a no hay

# ESTA NOCHE VOY A VERLA

Words and Music by
JUAN GABRIEL

# EL CUMBANCHERO

Words and Music by
RAFAEL HERNANDEZ

cum - ba, cum - ba, cum - ba, cum - ban - che - ro.

A bon - go, bon - go, bon - go, bon - go - se - ro.

# FEELINGS
## (¿Dime?)

English Words and Music by MORRIS ALBERT
and LOUIS GASTE
Spanish Words by THOMAS FUNDORA

# FLAMINGO

Lyric by ED ANDERSON
Music by TED GROUYA

# THE FOOL ON THE HILL

Words and Music by JOHN LENNON
and PAUL McCARTNEY

**Em7**  **A**  **D6**  **Bm**

No - bod - y seems to like __ him,  They can  tell what he wants. to do, _____  And
He nev - er lis - tens to __ them  He  knows  that they're __ the fools, _____

**Em7**  **A**  **Dm**  **Bb/D**  **Dm**

he nev - er shows his feel - ings, }  But  the  fool ___  on  the hill ___  sees  the sun __
They  don't like __ him,

**Bb/D**  **C**

___  go - ing down __  And  the  eyes ___  in his  head __  see the world __

**Dm(addE)**  **Dm7**  **1 D6**  **2 D6**

___  spin - ning  'round. __

**Repeat and Fade**

# FRENESÍ

Words and Music by
ALBERTO DOMINGUEZ

# GRANADA

Spanish Words and Music by AGUSTIN LARA
English Words by DOROTHY DODD

**Vigorously**

Gra - na - da, _____ I'm fall - ing un - der your spell, _____

_____ and if you could speak what a fas - ci - nat - ing tale you would tell: _____

_____ Of an age _____ the world has long for - got - ten, _____ of an

# THE GIFT!
## (Recado Bossa Nova)

Music by DJALMA FERREIRA
Original Lyric by LUIZ ANTONIO
English Lyric by PAUL FRANCIS WEBSTER

# GUADALAJARA

Words and Music by
PEPE GUIZAR

# GUANTANAMERA

Original lyrics and music by
JOSE FERNANDEZ DIAZ (JOSEITO FERNANDEZ)
Music adaptation by PETE SEEGER
Lyric adaptation by HECTOR ANGULO, based on a poem by JOSE MARTI

| | F | Bb | C7 | | F | Bb | C7 |

cre - ce la pal - ma,___ Y an-tes de mor-rir - me quie - ro, E - char mis
ill tow'rd each oth - er.___ This life will nev - er be hol - low To those who

*mf*

| F | Bb | C7 | F | Bb | C7 |

ver - sos del al - ma. Guan - ta-na-mer - a, gua - ji - ra
lis - ten and fol - low. Guan - ta-na-mer - a, I care a

*mp*

| F | Bb | C7 | F | Bb | C7 |

Guan - ta - na - mer - a. Guan - ta-na-mer - a, gua - ji - ra
lot for the la - dy! My in - spi - ra - tion, Guan - ta - na -

| F | Bb | **1, 2** C7 | F | **3** C7 | | F |

Guan - ta - na - mer - a. 2. Mi ver - so - a.
mo's fair - est la - dy! 2. I write my - dy.

## Spanish verses

1. Yo soy un hombre sincero,
   De donde crece la palma,
   Y antes de morirme quiero,
   Echar mis versos del alma.

2. Mi verso es de un verde claro,
   Y de un carmin encendido,
   Mi verso es un cierro herido,
   Que busca en el monte amparo.

3. Con los pobres de la tierra,
   Quiero yo mi suerte echar,
   El arroyo de la sierra,
   Me complace mas que el mar.

*NOTE - Repeat chorus after each of the above verses.*

## Literal translation

Guantanamera: A lady of Guantanamo
Guajira: Young woman

I'm a sincere man from the land of palms. Before dying, I wish to pour forth the poems of my soul.

My verses are soft green but also a flaming red. My verses are like wounded fauns seeking refuge in the forest.

I want to share my fate with the world's humble. A little mountain stream pleases me more than the ocean.

## English lyrics

1. I'm just a man who is trying -
   to do some good before dying,
   To ask each man and his brother -
   To bear no ill toward each other.
   This life will never be hollow -
   To those who listen and follow.

2. I write my rhymes with no learning,
   And yet with truth they are burning,
   But 'is the world waiting for them?
   Or will they all just ignore them?
   Have I a poet's illusion,
   A dream to die in seclusion? (Chorus)

3. A little brook on a mountain,
   The cooling spray of a fountain -
   Arouse in me an emotion, more
   than the vast boundless ocean,
   For there's a wealth beyond measure
   In little things that we treasure.
   (final Chorus, in Spanish)

# INOLVIDABLE

Words and Music by
JULIO GUTIERREZ

154

# IT'S IMPOSSIBLE
## (Somos Novios)

English Lyric by SID WAYNE
Spanish Words and Music by
ARMANDO MANZANERO

# LA CUCARACHA

Mexican Revolutionary Folksong

1. La Cu-ca-ra-cha, La Cu-ca-ra-cha, Run-ning up and down the
2. La Cu-ca-ra-cha, La Cu-ca-ra-cha, Wan-dered in a dress-ing
3. La Cu-ca-ra-cha, La Cu-ca-ra-cha, Met a lit-tle Pek-ing-
*La Cu-ca-ra-cha, La Cu-ca-ra-cha, Ya no pue-de ca-mi-*

house, La Cu-ca-ra-cha, La Cu-ca-ra-cha, Qui-et as a lit-tle
room,__ A love-ly la-dy, a pret-ty la-dy, Could-n't see well in the
nese,__ La Cu-ca-ra-cha, La Cu-ca-ra-cha, Bit his nose and made him
*nar,__ Por que no tie-ne, por que le fal-ta, Ma-ri-hua-na que fu-*

**4.**

La Cucaracha, La Cucaracha,
Woke up on election day,
La Cucaracha, La Cucaracha,
Heard the things they had to say,
A lot of lying and alibing,
Empty heads without a plan,
La Cucaracha, La Cucaracha,
Said, "I'm glad I'm not a man?"

*REFRAIN*

Then one day he saw an army,
Said, "The drums and bugle charm me,
Still if all the world are brothers,
Why should these men fight the others?
Guess it's just for love and glory,
Who'd believe another story?
These are men so brave and plucky,
Look at me, boy am I lucky!"

**5.**

La Cucaracha, La Cucaracha,
Wondered where his love could be,
La Cucaracha, La Cucaracha,
Wandered on so mis'rably.
The bees and beetles and old boll weevils,
Chased him off with many "Scats",
First they would scold him and then they told him,
They were bug aristocrats.

*REFRAIN*

Then one day while in the garden,
He just said, "I beg your pardon",
To a lady Cucaracha,
And he added, "Now I've gótcha."
She was coy but she was willing,
And for years their love was thrilling,
They still meet at half past seven,
Up in Cucaracha heaven.

La Cucaracha, La Cucaracha,
Just the same as you and I,
He got the jitters, the sweets and bitters,
Lived and loved and said "Goodbye."

# LA CUMPARSITA
## (The Masked One)

By G.H. MATOS RODRIGUEZ

# LAGRIMAS

Words and Music by MANUEL ALEJANDRO
and MARIA ALEJANDRA

# I GET IDEAS

Words by DORCAS COCHRAN
Music by JULIO C. SANDERS

# THE LOOK OF LOVE

## from CASINO ROYALE

Words by HAL DAVID
Music by BURT BACHARACH

Medium Rock Ballad (with much feeling)

The look ___ of love ___ is in ___
of love, ___ it's on ___

your eyes, ___ a look ___ your smile ___
your face, ___ a look ___ that time ___

can't dis - guise. ___ The look ___
can't e - rase. ___ Be mine ___

# LOVE ME WITH ALL YOUR HEART
## (Cuando Calienta El Sol)

Original Words and Music by CARLOS RIGUAL
and CARLOS A. MARTINOLI
English Words by SUNNY SKYLAR

Moderately slow, with firm beat

Love me with all your heart, ___ that's all I want, love; ___
*Cuan-do ca-lien-ta el sol ___ a-quí en la pla-ya,*

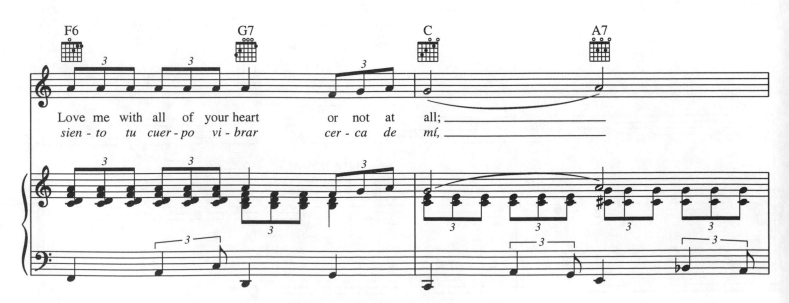

Love me with all of your heart or not at all; ___
*sien-to tu cuer-po vi-brar cer-ca de mí,*

# MALAGUEÑA
## from the Spanish Suite ANDALUCIA

Music and Spanish Lyric by
ERNESTO LECUONA
English Lyric by MARIAN BANKS

rit. poco — a tempo

mor hoy mi can - to so - lo es do - lor.

*colla parte* — *a tempo f*

8va loco

*p subito*

8va loco — 8va

*molto*

*dim. e poco rit.*

**Poco meno**

Ma - la - gue - ña de o - jos ne - gros,

8va

*mf*

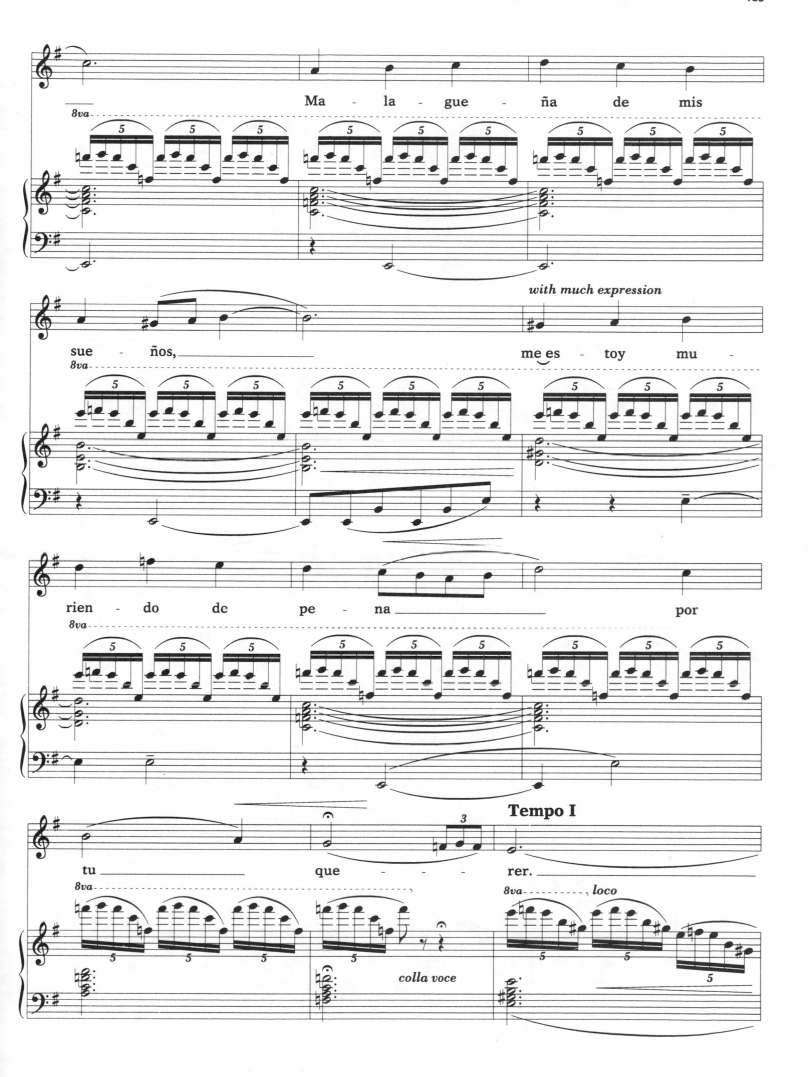

**Moderato**

Tra - la-ra-la-ra-la, tra-la-ra-la-rá, tra-la-ra-la-rá-la-rá-la-rá-la-

rá!

Ah ___ Ah ___ Ah ___ Ah ___

**Vivace**

# MAMBO JAMBO
## (Que Rico El Mambo)

English Words by RAYMOND KARL and CHARLIE TOWNE
Original Words and Music by DAMASO PEREZ PRADO

# MAMBO #5

Words and Music by
DAMASO PEREZ PRADO

**Moderately**

# MARIA ELENA

English Lyrics by S.K. RUSSELL
Music and Spanish Lyrics by LORENZO BARCELATA

# MAS QUE NADA

Words and Music by
JORGE BEN

# MI MAGDALENA

Words and Music by
CHUCHO MARTINEZ GIL

# MEXICAN HAT DANCE
## (Jarabe Topatio)

By F.A. PARTICHELA

Tempo primo

# MIAMI BEACH RUMBA

Words by ALBERT GAMSE
Music by IRVING FIELDS

Rhumba

I start-ed out to go to Hai- ti,    Soon I was at Mi- am- i
That's where the or- ang- es are round- er,    That's where the win- ter days are

Beach.    There, not so ver- y far from Hai- ti,
warm.    That's where I caught a hun- dred pound- er,

# NOCHE DE RONDA
## (Be Mine Tonight)

Original Words and Music by MARIA TERESA LARA
English Words by SUNNY SKYLAR

# NEVER ON SUNDAY

from Jules Dassin's Motion Picture NEVER ON SUNDAY

Words by BILLY TOWNE
Music by MANOS HADJIDAKIS

# OBSESIÓN

Words and Music by
PEDRO FLORES

**Lento**

Por al- to es- té el cie- lo en el mun- do, por hon- do que es- té el mar pro- fun- do, no ha- brá u- na ba- rre- ra en el mun- do que un a- mor pro-

# ONLY ONCE IN MY LIFE
## (Solamente Una Vez)

Music and Spanish Words by AGUSTIN LARA
English Words by RICK CARNES and JANIS CARNES

# OUR LANGUAGE OF LOVE
## from IRMA LA DOUCE

Music by MARGUERITE MONNOT
Original French words by ALEXANDRE BREFFORT
English words by JULIAN MORE, DAVID HENEKER and MONTY NORMAN

# THE PEANUT VENDOR
## (El Manisero)

English Words by MARION SUNSHINE and L. WOLFE GILBERT
Music and Spanish Words by MOISES SIMONS

# POR AMOR

Words and Music by
RAFAEL SOLANO

# PERFIDIA

Words and Music by
ALBERTO DOMINGUEZ

249

# POINCIANA
## (Song of the Tree)

Words by BUDDY BERNIER
Music by NAT SIMON

# POR ELLA

Words and Music by JULIO IGLESIAS,
RAMON ARCUSA and MANUEL DE LA CALVA

sé sin es - pe - rar - lo de don Juan a con - quis - ta - do fue
vi da en blan - co y ne - gro se vis tió en co - lo - res neu - vos fue } por
bié tan - to de pron - to y me e - na - mo - ré del to - do fue
to - dos se pre - gun - tan por quién can - to mi a - mar - gu - ra es }

**Cmaj7**

el - la.___

**1,3**
**A7b9**

Por

**2,4**
**Gm7** **C7**

Por

**Fmaj7**

el - la.___

{ Sé que me mue - ro por
{ Tan - tos «Te quie - ros» por

**Cmaj7**

el - la___ ~
el - la___ ~

{ to - do lo he si - do } por
{ tan - tos re - cuer - dos } por

# QUIZÁS, QUIZÁS, QUIZÁS
## (Perhaps, Perhaps, Perhaps)

Music and Spanish Words by
OSVALDO FARRES
English Words by JOE DAVIS

# QUIERO DORMIR CANSADO

Words and Music by MANUEL ALEJANDRO
and ANA MAGDALENA

Quie-ro dor-mir__ can-sa-do pa-ra no pen-sar en tí;__
Quie-ro dor-mir__ can-sa-do y no des-per-tar ja-más;__

quie-ro dor-mir__ pro-fun - da-men - te
quie-ro dor-mir__ e - ter - na men - te

# SABOR A MÍ
## (Be True to Me)

Original Words and Music by ALVARO CARRILLO
English Words by MEL MITCHELL

Tan - to tiem - po dis - fru - ta - mos es - te a - mor, _____ nues - tras al - mas se a - cer -
If I prove how much I love you with each kiss, _____ will you cross your heart and

ca - ron tan - to a - sí _____ que yo guar - do tu sa - bor pe - ro tú lle - vas tam -
prom - ise this _____ that it's more than just a thrill, that you love me and you

bién sa - bor a mi. _____ Si ne - ga - ras mi pre -
will be true to me. _____ I will give you all my

# SAMBA DE ORFEU

Words by ANTONIO MARIA
Music by LUIZ BONFA

# SIN REMEDIO

Words and Music by
JESUS CHUCHO NAVARRO

# SLIGHTLY OUT OF TUNE
## (Desafinado)

English Lyric by JON HENDRICKS and JESSIE CAVANAUGH
Original Text by NEWTON MENDONCA
Music by ANTONIO CARLOS JOBIM

# SIN UN AMOR

Words and Music by ALFREDO GIL
and JESUS CHUCHO NAVARRO

Sin un a - mor

# SPANISH EYES

Words by CHARLES SINGLETON and EDDIE SNYDER
Music by BERT KAEMPFERT

# SWAY
## (Quien Sera)

English Words by NORMAN GIMBEL
Spanish Words and Music by PABLO BELTRAN RUIZ

# TRES PALABRAS
## (Without You)

Original Words and Music by OSVALDO FARRES
English Words by RAY GILBERT

# TICO TICO
## (Tico No Fuba)

Words and Music by ZEQUINHA ABREU,
ALOYSIO OLIVEIRA and ERVIN DRAKE

**Bright Samba**

Oh ti-co-ti-co tick! __ Oh ti-co-ti-co tock! __ This ti-co-
*O ti-co-ti-co tá, __ tá ou-tra vez a-qui, __ o ti-co-*

ti-co he's the cuck-oo in my clock. And when he says: "Cuck - oo!" __ he means it's
*ti-co-tá co-men-do o meu fu-bá. Si o ti-co-ti-co tem, __ tem que se a-*

time to woo; __ It's "Ti-co-time" for all the lov-ers in the
*li-men - tar, __ Que vá co - mer u-mas mi-nho-cas no po-*

# TIME WAS

English Words by S.K. RUSSELL
Music by MIGUEL PRADO

# TU FELICIDAD
## (Made for Each Other)

Original Words and Music by
RENE TOUZET
English Words by ERVIN DRAKE and JIMMY SHIRL

# VOY A APAGAR LA LUZ

Words and Music by
ARMANDO MANZANERO

# USTED

Music by GABRIEL RUIZ
Words by JOSE ANTONIO ZORRILLA

# WHAT A DIFF'RENCE A DAY MADE

English Words by STANLEY ADAMS
Music and Spanish Words by
MARIA GREVER